TANLEY GIBBONS STAMP COLLECTING SE

C000010845

STAMP COLLECTING
HOW TO START

AMES WATSON

STANLEY GIBBONS PUBLICATIONS LTD
399 STRAND, LONDON WC2R 0LX

By Appointment to H.M. The Queen
Stanley Gibbons Ltd, London
Philatelists

© *Stanley Gibbons Publications Ltd 1983*

First Published 1983

The Author: James Watson joined the staff of Stanley Gibbons in 1946 and worked in the New Issues Dept. before becoming a feature writer for Gibbons Stamp Monthly. He retired from Gibbons in 1981 but still contributes his regular feature 'Panorama' for the magazine. Mr. Watson has written several books on philately—most notably the Stanley Gibbons Book of Stamps and Stamp Collecting. He has also written about cine photography and is an expert on picture postcards of the early 20th century.

Designed by Julia Lilauwala.

Printed in Great Britain by BAS Printers Limited, Over Wallop, Hampshire.

ISBN 0 85259 039 3

Item No. 2760

CONTENTS

INTRODUCTION

Starting a stamp collection is rather like learning to swim. You practise the elementary strokes at the shallow end, getting the feel of the water and striving to keep afloat. Eventually you gain confidence, learn more advanced strokes and have the courage to plunge into the deep end of the pool. Just as the swimmer had the compulsion and ability to learn, so should the embryo stamp collector be motivated to read, mark and learn about stamps before taking the plunge'. It's fun starting a collection and finding out all about the stamps which have been issued by the countries of the world over the years. Postage stamps are miniature works of art—colourful, well-designed and superbly printed. Some of them commemorate famous people and events, others show animals and birds, fishes and flowers, railways, ships and aeroplanes, buildings and bridges, coats-of-arms and flags, achievements in space and in sport.

Stamps are educational and provide some of the nicest—and most practical—ways of learning geography and history, politics and religion, and the everyday way of life in different parts of the world. Through stamps you can also learn about the postal services and a country's postal history and transport systems, the interest and significance of postmarks, and the modern craze for 'covers' (postmarked envelopes), especially 'first day covers'. But before you buy a single stamp—or large packet of stamps which you may later regret—it is recommended that you try and get hold of a *Gibbons Simplified Catalogue of Stamps of the World* and see for yourself the enormous number and variety of stamps which have been issued so far. Again, before you buy, try and see as many stamps as you can—in dealers' showcases, stock-books and shop windows, and in displays at stamp exhibitions and fairs. Only in this way can you feel confident enough to undertake the 'breast-strokes' of philately, and decide which, of all the stamps you have seen, appeal to you most of all. There is more, much more, to the hobby of stamp collecting than sticking stamps in an album. This you will learn as you gradually acquire stamps and study them.

YOUR FIRST STAMPS

The usual advice—very good advice—to the novice is to buy 'the largest packet of whole-world stamps you can afford', together with a medium-priced album and some gummed 'hinges' to mount the stamps in it. This simple start will be your 'apprenticeship', and you will have the pleasure of sorting the stamps by country and arranging them in the album. You will be able to identify most of the stamps without hesitation: put aside any which you are doubtful about until you can trace them in the catalogue. A companion volume in this series—*Stamp Collecting—How to Identify Stamps*—will help you to recognise foreign country names and inscriptions. To keep your interest alive, you will be seeking more and more stamps, and there are numerous sources of supply.

Your family and business friends may receive letters from abroad and may be persuaded to save the stamps for you. Even Guernsey, Jersey and the Isle of Man have their own distinctive pictorial stamps which are well worth collecting. You can buy additional packets of stamps to augment your collection, and if you buy one of the stamp magazines you will find on the bookstalls, you will see among the advertisements that some dealers offer to send stamps 'on approval'. You can examine the stamps at leisure in your own home, keep those you wish to purchase and pay for them when you return the remainder. Certain dealers make up special selections of cheap and attractive stamps for beginners, and you would be expected to spend a reasonable amount—say £2 to £5—and return the unwanted stamps promptly.

At this stage some of your stamps will be unused, others postally used, and it is usual to collect one or the other, not both. Mixed unused and used stamps look rather a hotchpotch in the album, while a page of unused stamps, neatly arranged, can be very attractive. However, your preference may be for 'fine used' (i.e. lightly postmarked) stamps which you can obtain from letters in the mails at little cost. Unused stamps usually cost more as one has to pay the face value of the stamps plus the dealer's usual commission or profit. On the other hand, some stamps—especially those from the more remote British Commonwealth territories—are quite scarce in postally used condition and cost more than unused ones.

2 Coastal scenery and buildings are featured on many Channel Islands and Manx issues

Some recruits to the hobby are fortunate enough to inherit an existing stamp collection which provides a ready-made start and a foundation on which to build an even larger collection. Alternatively a section of it—which has the most appeal—can be kept, and the remainder sold off to a stamp dealer or at auction, using the proceeds to buy the stamps you want. Others take a header into the deep end and buy a second-hand collection, either from a dealer or at auction, which can be sorted, rearranged, augmented or broken up at will. Most auction sales have collections and mixed lots on offer and you can find the details of forthcoming sales in stamp magazines.

Whether you buy collections or packets you are bound to acquire a good percentage of common stamps—usually low-value stamps which may have been issued and used by the million. Instinct and the stamp catalogue will tell you which these are, but don't discard them too hastily. You may, at a later date, switch to collecting only the stamps of a certain country or group of countries where even the common stamps may be needed to form the nucleus of a collection. Also, do not be too concerned with the *value* of your stamps— remember that you are (or should be) collecting them for enjoyment and not with the vain hope of making a fortune! Some stamps are more valuable than others and many increase in value over the years, but factors such as condition and capricious supply and demand affect stamp values.

Condition—that is, *good* condition—is vitally important. Nothing detracts more from the value of a stamp than a crease, a tear, a stain or a heavy postmark. Damaged stamps are usually worthless and should be discarded or replaced as soon as possible. Unused stamps should have their original gum as issued in 'mint' condition by the post office, though traces of the use of a gummed hinge are generally acceptable. The ideal postmark is light (not faint) and clear, a circular town datestamp being preferable to part of a slogan cancellation. Heavy black cancellations which obliterate the stamp's design are entirely unacceptable. Some postmarks—early types (say, prior to 1920), military camps, railway stations and ship cancellations etc.—are often more valuable than the stamps, especially if kept intact on the original cover.

3 Only keep used stamps with clear postmarks, stamps with heavy cancellations should be avoided

ONE-COUNTRY STYLE

About 300 countries in the world currently issue postage stamps—'definitive' or ordinary stamps for everyday use and commemoratives or 'special event' stamps for anniversaries, national and local celebrities or occasions. The great dominions of Australia, Canada, India and South Africa were formed of provinces and states, each of which issued their own stamps years ago. New stamps are issued at the rate of about 6,000 a year, so that the total number of stamps issued all over the world to date is truly vast—well over 210,000 even on a simplified basis. Thus it is impossible for the collector to form a complete whole-world collection: difficult enough to complete even a representative one. But you should still persevere with your whole-world collection, getting to know as many different stamps as you can, until such time as you feel that you are ready to 'branch out' which, oddly enough, means concentrating upon the stamps of a certain country or group of countries.

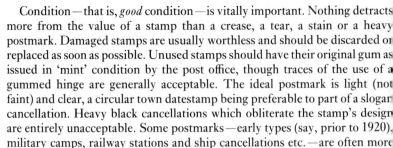

4 Modern definitive (small size) and commemorative (large size) stamps

From the famous Penny Black to the attractive issues of today, the stamps of Great Britain are understandably popular with collectors. Every new issue inspires more people to collect 'GB' stamps. Some become interested in the earlier stamps which already have a large following, and there is a constant demand for Victorian, Edwardian and Georgian stamps. Those who began collecting Elizabethan stamps at the commencement of the present reign in 1952, and who have kept their collections up to date with all the subsequent issues, now have about 700 different stamps, definitives and commemoratives, in their albums.

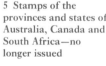

5 Stamps of the provinces and states of Australia, Canada and South Africa—no longer issued

6 British Victorian, Edwardian and Georgian stamps— popular with collectors worldwide

7 Royal events have featured on British commemoratives—the Coronation (1953) and Royal Weddings (1981, 1973)

For many years now the British Post Office has encouraged and stimulated stamp collecting with its regular issues of attractive pictorial stamps—usually six or seven special issues each year—accompanied by appropriate 'first day' covers and postmarks, presentation packs and postcard reproductions of the stamps. Special facilities—and in some instances, back issues of commemorative stamps—are provided by the philatelic counters at numerous post offices throughout the country, and at the Philatelic Bureau in Edinburgh, where a credit account may be maintained to cover the cost of future issues. A monthly magazine, the *Philatelic Bulletin*, is published by the British Post Office.

8 A 'First Day of Issue' postmark—these were introduced in 1963

9 Machin £sd and decimal stamps. The 'Machins' were introduced in 1967

You can start a G.B. collection any way you wish, according to the amount you want to spend—it's a good idea to budget for a fixed sum of 'spending money' on your stamps each month. Any cash in hand at the end of a particular month can be carried forward, contributing to more substantial purchases. Here are two suggestions for 'starters': buy the current G.B. commemorative or special issue and look out for forthcoming issues, also building up a long set of the current 'Machin' definitive stamps which range from ½p to £5 face value. These stamps were designed after a plaster cast of the Queen's head by Arnold Machin, the sculptor, and they were first issued in the old 'pence and shillings' face values in 1967. The decimal Machins were introduced in 1971 and already some of the stamps are obsolete as postal rates have changed and there has been no postal need for certain denominations. Also remember that a change of design is possible after a number of years.

10 Common stamps of Victoria, George V and Edward VIII and the first British commemorative

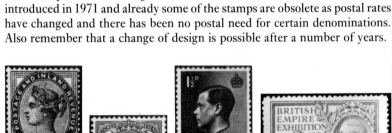

My second suggestion takes us back to 'square one'—buy a large packet of mixed G.B. stamps: usually a packet of 500 all-different postally used G.B. costs about £5, while 200 different commemoratives would cost the same or a little more. These packets contain fairly common stamps from all reigns—Queen Victoria, King Edward VII, King George V, King George VI, possibly the four stamps of King Edward VIII, and Queen Elizabeth II. The first British commemoratives were the British Empire Exhibition (Wembley) stamps of 1924 and there have been about 150 special issues since that time.

The 'one-country' idea can be extended to any country in the world. Canada and New Zealand are among the most popular countries, while the smaller British Commonwealth territories such as Anguilla, Barbados, Cyprus, Fiji and Gibraltar all have their loyal followers. In Europe some of the most entertaining stamps come from France, Germany, Holland and Switzerland, while the issues of Israel, Japan and some of the modern African states are full of historical interest for the collector. The stamps of the United States represent every national and international anniversary, cause and event in bold, colourful designs with a constantly-changing pictorial series of definitives. The new stamps from most countries can be obtained by subscription to a new issue service.

11 American stamps popular with collectors. Subjects range from flowers to space exploration

MANY KINDS OF STAMPS

12 'Postage Revenue' stamp—valid for both postal and fiscal use

At an early stage one should know about the different kinds of stamps in general use, some for special purposes connected with postal operations, others having no postal validity at all. Definitive and commemorative stamps have already been explained: however, there are variations which require explanation, remembering that we are primarily concerned with *postage* stamps. Definitives are often inscribed 'Postage and Revenue' which means that they can also be used for fiscal or public revenue purposes, on bills and documents, licences, receipts and telegrams. Such stamps sometimes find their way into mixed packets and, if you can identify them by the pen-marks or rubber stamps used to cancel them, should be 'weeded out'. On the other hand there are fiscal stamps inscribed 'REVENUE' only and some people collect these as a sideline.

Charity or 'semi-postal' stamps are usually commemoratives bearing an additional premium or surcharge which is accumulated by the post office and handed over to the charity—perhaps the International Red Cross or one of the campaign funds for the treatment of cancer, leprosy, tuberculosis and other diseases—to be used in medical research and the maintenance of hospitals etc. Some stamps, definitive and commemorative, are additionally inscribed 'AIR' or 'AIRMAIL' and usually bear the appropriate face value for the specific airmail fee. Their purpose, however, is rather outdated as ordinary definitives can be used on airmail letters, and airmail stamps are accepted on ordinary letters. Air stamps of France and French-speaking countries usually bear the words 'Poste Aerienne'; Austria, 'Flugpost'; Germany and the Scandinavian countries, 'Luftpost'. Spain and the Spanish-orientated Latin-American countries use 'Correo Aereo'; Portugal (and Brazil), 'Aereo' or 'Correio Aereo'; Italy, 'Posta Aerea'. Dutch airmail stamps are inscribed 'Luchtpost'; Hungarian, 'Legiposta'.

13 Charity stamps from Belgium, New Zealand and Switzerland

14 Air mail stamps— variously inscribed 'Poste Aerienne', 'Flugpost', etc.

15 Stamps for special purposes—Postage Due and To Pay issues

In the early days of the posts, the postal charges were collected at the time of delivery of the letters, a tedious and troublesome task for the letter-carriers. Then Rowland Hill introduced the prepayment of postage and the world's first postage stamps, thereby reducing the problem of unpaid and undeliverable letters. Later, unstamped letters were charged to the recipient at double the deficiency, and in 1914 the British Post Office introduced special 'Postage Due' stamps for use on unstamped or insufficiently-stamped letters. Thus an unstamped letter is stamped with a postage due equivalent to twice the unpaid postage, and postmarked by the postal staff as a kind of advance receipt for payment of the deficiency which is collected from the adressee on delivery. French postage dues are inscribed 'Timbre Taxe', while 'Porto' is used by several countries. Polish dues are identified by 'Doplata', and the Dutch version is 'Te Betalen—Port'.

16 Stamps for special purposes—official mail

Official stamps are used by Government departments and may be inscribed or overprinted 'Official' or, as in India and Pakistan, 'Service'. Foreign versions are 'Officiel' or 'Oficial', 'Dienstmarke' (Germany), 'Offentlig sak' or 'Off. sak' or simply 'O.S.' (Norway), while Belgium's railway officials bear the ornamental letter 'B'. At one time British stamps were overprinted 'Army Official', 'Board of Education', 'I.R. Official' (Inland Revenue) etc., while Canada had official stamps overprinted 'O.H.M.S.' or 'G' (for 'Government') between 1949 and 1963. The current officials and postage dues are not sold over the post office counter, but can generally be obtained, unused, through a country's philatelic bureau.

17 Stamps for special purposes—Express and Registered posts

Some countries use Express and Special Delivery stamps to cover the extra fees for these services. These may be inscribed 'Urgente', 'Extra Rapido' or 'Entrega Inmediata' in Spain and some Latin-American countries, while

'Espresso' is used in Italy. Among the 'special-purpose' stamps which are seldom seen today are those for newspapers, parcels and registration (for registered letters), also telegraph stamps used for the prepayment of telegrams. These and some other revenue types were sometimes used postally and are then known as 'postal-fiscals'.

18 Provisional stamps overprinted for change in country name. War Tax Stamps

'Provisional' stamps include those overprinted with a new country name (such as 'Sabah' on North Borneo) or surcharged with new values to make good temporary shortages of certain denominations. Stamps inscribed or overprinted 'War' or 'War Tax' were issued by some Commonwealth countries during World War I to raise funds to finance their military commitments. 'Obligatory Tax' stamps are issued to collect funds for national or charitable purposes — they have no postal validity, but their use is usually compulsory in addition to the ordinary postage stamps.

THE STAMP COLLECTOR'S BIBLE

The stamp catalogue, basically a dealer's price-list, is a most essential work of reference for the stamp collector. It provides complete, detailed lists of all the postage stamps issued by every country in the world from the earliest days, with information about dates of issue, commemorative events, face values, colours and designs, and — if it is a fairly new catalogue — the current prices of the stamps, unused and postally used. For the beginner and general collector the most useful catalogue is the *Stanley Gibbons Simplified Catalogue of Stamps of the World* which, now in two volumes, has just replaced the former 'Stamps of the World'. It contains all the details — except perforations, watermarks, designers, printers and varieties — the average collector needs for every country, but it is rather expensive for a young collector. If current stamp values are not of importance then one can buy a second-hand catalogue at a much reduced price: alternatively, most public libraries have a range of *Gibbons Catalogues* which can be referred to or borrowed.

Countries in the 'Simplified' are arranged in alphabetical order — Abu Dhabi to Zululand — and under each country heading there are brief notes about its location, status and currency. The stamp illustrations are actual size (British Commonwealth) or reduced to $\frac{3}{4}$ size (Foreign Countries) and usually only one example of a set is shown, although all the different designs are recorded. Below the illustration appears the main heading which gives the year of issue and, in the case of commemorative issues, the nature of the person or event commemorated. There follows the tabulated list of stamps —

catalogue number, 'type' number (if the stamp is illustrated), face value and colours and/or design, and two columns of prices. The first column shows the unused price, and the second column the used price of the stamp. These are the prices you can expect to pay for the stamps from a dealer, although in some circumstances you may obtain them at a discount on the catalogue prices, while of course common stamps in packets cost much less than listed prices.

19 Stanley Gibbons *Simplified* catalogue— published annually for nearly half a century

The world-famous *Gibbons Catalogue* was first published by Edward Stanley Gibbons as a penny price-list in 1865. The main catalogue now comprises 22 Parts and is intended for the more advanced collector—*Part 1* is the famous *British Commonwealth Catalogue*, which includes all British and Commonwealth stamps from the earliest issues to the present time. Of the remaining parts, ten are devoted to European countries and eleven to overseas countries. The *Elizabethan Specialised Stamp Catalogue*, as its name implies, deals exclusively with the stamps of the present reign for all territories within the Commonwealth. In addition it lists and illustrates all the known printing flaws and errors on Elizabethan stamps. For the specialist GB collector Gibbons also publish the *Great Britain Specialised Catalogue* in four volumes. The '*Simplified*', *Part 1* and *Elizabethan* are published, fully updated, in the autumn each year—the others have new editions occasionally as required.

20 The cover of the first S.G. pricelist (1865) featured on a stamp from Ajman

21 Stanley Gibbons
Part 1 and Elizabethan
catalogues—two of the
most popular in the
Gibbons range

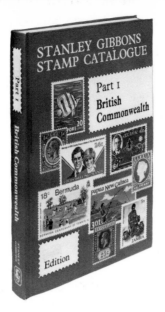
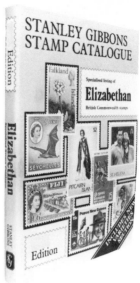

For the GB collector who wishes to economise and yet keep in touch with the latest market values of his stamps, Stanley Gibbons publish three admirable 'mini-catalogues' or checklists—*Collect British Stamps*, *Collect Channel Islands Stamps* and *Collect Isle of Man Stamps*. These are modestly-priced booklets which appear every six months or so, showing all the new issues and latest prices since previous editions. The stamps are illustrated in colour, and first day covers, presentation packs, officials and postage dues are included. Many GB collectors take an interest in varieties of watermark—inverted, reversed and sideways etc.—and *CBS* includes a special list of them.

22 Two of the popular
'Collect' series

As you progress in the hobby so the catalogue will become of more and more assistance. It shows you which stamps you need to complete a set, their face values and their designs, thus providing a guide to the arrangement of your stamps in the album. The catalogue will also help you to become acquainted with colours and their names—the basic reds, blues and greens of the '*Simplified*' or the more explicit carmine-reds, greenish blues and yellow-greens of the main catalogues. Eventually you will probably select GB or some other country or group of countries as your especial favourites in a more specialised way, when you will need an even more detailed and specialised catalogue. Remember, too, that Gibbons' catalogue numbers are used the world over—they serve to identify stamps for dealers and collectors—the former in their advertisements, the latter when negotiating 'swaps' with fellow collectors.

THE COLLECTOR'S TOOL-BOX

A book—such as a dictionary—which is in constant use soon begins to show signs of wear. The edges of the pages gradually lose their crisp, fresh looks, and the same thing happens to your stamps with excessive handling. Thus your first essential item of equipment should be a pair of stamp tweezers—these are made of light, plated metal with slender, flattened tips or 'spade' ends enabling stamps to be picked up and sorted quickly and surely. With a little practice, tweezers are easy to handle (held with the hilt in the palm of your hand), and they are usually supplied in plastic cases so that you can carry them around in your pocket.

STANLEY GIBBONS *Instanta*
PERFORATION GAUGE
Patent 573065   Made in England

23 *above* Gibbons 'Instanta' perforation gauge; *left* Magnifying glasses come in a variety of styles—every collector should have one

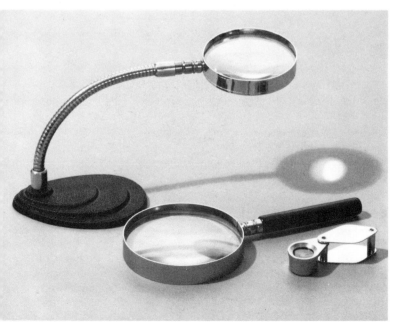

The magnifying glass is the one tool which everyone associates with stamp collecting. Through the magnifying glass stamp designs appear in detailed close-up and are seen to be miniature works of art. You can see the lines or cuts which make up a portrait or scene on an engraved stamp, or study the quality and peculiarities of the other printing processes—the graduated 'dots' of photogravure or the smooth honeycomb background of lithographed stamps. You will also enjoy looking for errors and varieties, many of which are visible only through a glass. There are folding magnifiers for the pocket, stand or 'box' types which are free-standing while you arrange the stamps or make notes, illuminated magnifiers and high-powered glasses for the specialist.

Perforations and watermarks will eventually concern you—differences to the normal perforation or watermark of a stamp can enhance its value, and it is necessary to be able to measure the perforation or identify the watermark if only to establish that you have the normal stamp. The perforation gauge measures the number of perforations within the measure of 2 centimetres. Perforations are a stamp's 'teeth' and their measurements vary according to the type of perforating machine used. Often the stamp's top and bottom 'perfs' differ from those at the sides (called a 'compound perforation'), and measurements range from 7 (large holes) to about 18 (small holes). The 'Instanta' is a kind of slide-rule perforation gauge—other types have the various measurements, in rows of appropriately-sized dots, printed or engraved on card or plastic.

24 Gibbons Colour
Key—your guide to
stamp colours.

The main instrument for detecting stamp watermarks is the human eye! The watermark is simply a thinning of the paper in the form of letters or an emblem such as a crown, and it can usually be seen when the stamp is held with the light shining through it, or if the stamp is placed face down on a dark—preferably black—surface, remembering that the watermark is 'right way round' when viewed through the front, and in reverse when viewed through the back. If a watermark is known to exist on a particular stamp and it is still not visible, then we have to use scientific aids—the benzine-dropper and watermark tray or tile, or one of the proprietory detectors. The stamp will surely reveal its dark secret when it is placed face down on the black tray and splashed with a few drops of benzine (*not* benzene)—be alert because the benzine evaporates almost instantly, and be careful because it is also highly inflammable. Modern British stamps no longer have watermarks.

Another kind of gauge, one which enables you to chart flaws and varieties on stamps through a plastic transparent grid, is the 'Thirkell' Position Finder. It pinpoints their location and provides a useful reference for other collectors. If colours or colour-names are a problem, then *Gibbons Colour Guide* will assist you. It is a folder containing samples of the hundred colours most helpful for the identification and naming of particular stamps, and it offers guidance on distinguishing shades. A more elaborate guide is the novel *Gibbons Colour Key* which contains 200 colour tabs, including many of the shades most likely to be encountered.

Our tool-box is now almost completely filled. There are gadget-boxes for removing the paper from stamps clipped from envelopes etc., but it is simpler and safer to invest in a plastic tray—shallow with raised sides—say 12″ × 9″ or larger, fill it with lukewarm water and lay your clippings on the surface, stamps face upwards. After 10 minutes or so you will be able to 'float' the stamps off the paper and dry them between sheets of clean blotting-paper. This is generally more convenient than commandeering the bathroom! You will need gummed hinges, too, to mount your stamps in the album. Carry on reading!

YOUR ALBUM CHOICE

Before you purchase your first stamp album you should have some plan in your mind, even just a few thoughts and inclinations, on the likely progress and eventual scope of your collection. If, like many beginners, you buy or are given a monster packet of stamps and a printed album with a page for every country, then probably no 'pearls of wisdom' on my part will prevent you from sticking the stamps in it so that you can satisfy yourself—and your friends—that you are now the proud owner of a 'stamp collection'. Sooner or later you will run out of space and the surplus stamps of some countries will be scattered untidily on other pages. In these circumstances enthusiasm wanes, interest flags and the only solution is a larger album with all the work of rearranging your stamps.

Start right! As you begin to accumulate stamps, you should acquire one of the popular 'slip-in' collecting books or one of the stock-books such as stamp dealers use to keep your stamps in order and in good condition. These have strips or pockets on every page and you simply slip your stamps into them, arranged in order of country or as you wish. Some collectors use stock-books permanently for convenience, but of course the stamps are not displayed as they would be in an album. It is time to think of an album only when your stock-book is reasonably full and you have decided to build up a general collection (necessitating a large whole-world album), or concentrate on the stamps of one or two countries (blank loose-leaf or 'one-country' albums).

25 Albums suitable for
young collectors

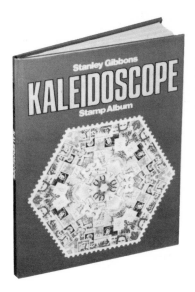
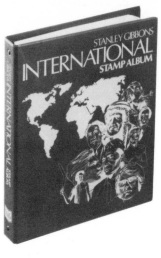

Your choice of a suitable album is important. It shouldn't be too small—for the reasons stated above—and not too large because, unless you have a very large collection and anticipate buying many more stamps, your existing stamps will be greatly extended and give your collection a sparse appearance. Printed albums—those with printed country headings at the top of each page—can be obtained fastbound (like a book) or with loose-leaf ring-fitting binders. The great advantage of the loose-leaf system is that the leaves can be rearranged—and extra leaves added—as you wish. The 'one-country' printed albums usually have a space for each stamp, possibly illustrated, with periodic supplements.

The Gibbons' range of one-country albums includes Great Britain, the Channel Islands and the Isle of Man, specially designed for straightforward collections of those popular countries, while there are also similar albums for Australia, Canada and New Zealand. All of these albums are also available in 'Hingeless' versions—that is they have transparent mounts already affixed over the illustrations of the stamps so that you only need to slot in your stamps. Obviously the affixing of the mounts by hand is a time-consuming process and hence such albums are more expensive than those which require you to affix the mounts yourself. For many collectors the convenience is well worth the extra outlay. The advantage of using transparent mounts is set out below (*Arranging Your Stamps*). The Windsor album is supplied with a springback binder, with printed spaces for all G.B. stamps, a guiding catalogue listing and regular supplements to keep the album up to date. For the 'do-it-yourself' collector who prefers to arrange and 'write-up' the collection on blank leaves there are many splendid albums in the Gibbons range to choose from. They are priced according to quality, size and capacity, and the binders are springback (which open wide to release the leaves), ring-fitting or peg-fitting.

Multi-ring albums have the advantage of lying flat when the album is opened, while it is usually necessary to take out spring-back and peg-fitted leaves when working on them, i.e. arranging the stamps and writing-up. You can prepare your own country headings etc. for blank leaves, or you can buy the special booklets of gummed country-name labels. Blank albums are of course especially suitable for thematic collecting—the pursuit of a certain subject or theme (such as birds, flowers or transport)—where the arrangement of the stamps entirely depends on the theme and its sub-divisions. More details of thematic collecting can be found in another in this series—*Stamp Collecting—Collecting By Theme*. It suggests many attractive pictorial themes and describes how you can form an attractive and entertaining subject collection.

26 The Gibbons *One-Country* albums—spaces provided for all basic stamps

There are numerous albums for first day covers and airmail flown covers, for stamp booklets and for picture postcards, including the large Post Office stamp cards. However, your main concern must now be the choice of your first stamp album and you should visit your local stamp shop to see what is available. If you live within easy reach of London, then it would be sensible to make the trip and visit 'Gibbons in the Strand' or one of the other stamp stores where you will probably have a much wider selection. Most of our principal towns and cities have well-established stamp shops, but if you live in a remote area you can buy from Stanley Gibbons by mail-order. The convenience will justify the postage. Ask for an illustrated price-list!

27 Cover Albums.

ARRANGING YOUR STAMPS

The essence of a good stamp arrangement is neatness—stamps placed squarely in the spaces provided for them or in level, tidy rows on a blank leaf. It sounds simple—and indeed it is—but it does require care and thought. Some printed albums have stamp 'squares' in rows across the album page. Usually these are big enough to accommodate the majority of stamps which are invariably rectangular—horizontal or vertical—in shape. Larger stamps will extend beyond the confines of the square and in such cases the printed background should be ignored, with two stamps taking up the space of three squares. Personal preference and ingenuity should be employed! Some printed albums have provision for stamps on both sides of the leaf and the danger here is that stamps on facing pages will tangle with each other and may become damaged. Where transparent interleaving is not provided, it can be purchased, or some other form of thin paper—typing copy paper, for example—can be lightly gummed between leaves, close to the spine.

For the average collection, gummed stamp hinges are the most convenient to use. These are small slips of gummed paper which attach the stamp to the album page—just fold down about a quarter of the hinge, gummed side outwards, and lightly moisten the narrow folded portion with the tip of your little finger: if you use your tongue to lick the hinge there is the danger of wetting the stamp as well. Attach this portion to the back of the stamp at the top, just below the perforations, and then moisten the lower part of the 'flap' and place the stamp in its appropriate place and press down. The best hinges are 'peelable', but only after they have completely dried out, so if the stamp is crooked or in the wrong place, leave it awhile before attempting to remove it, otherwise you may rip off the back of the stamp or part of the album page.

The alternative to using hinges is the system of gummed 'pockets' or strips—'Showgard', 'S.G. Hawid' or 'S.G. Gard' mounts—which employ the 'slip in' principle (rather like your stock-book) with transparent fronts and black backing, tailored to fit your stamp and sold in convenient singles or strips. The advantage of these is that you can keep your unused stamps in pristine mint condition, which some collectors (and dealers) consider to be essential in the event of re-sale.

Whichever method of mounting the stamps on the blank album leaf is used, the basic principles are the same (although the gummed strips may take up more 'stamp space') in arranging them—neat, orderly rows of, say, five or six stamps, depending on their size and format, and perhaps six or more rows to a page. Each page should be carefully planned to ascertain how many stamps you will get on a page without overcrowding. A certain group or set of stamps may be incomplete and you should allow spaces for the missing ones if you have a reasonable chance of obtaining them. A completed page looks good and is a source of satisfaction. So-called blank leaves are not strictly blank— they have an imprinted quadrille pattern (like graph paper) which, with the aid of light pencil marks, enables you to plan level rows of stamps, positioned with equal spaces between them and at the beginning and end of each row.

The monotony of page after page of uniform rows of stamps can be avoided by paying attention to balance and symmetry—the 'lozenge' pattern, with short rows at top and bottom of the page, or the 'hourglass' arrangement with the shorter rows in the centre, like a 'waist'. Bizarre and fanciful layouts should be avoided—invariably they waste space and lack symmetrical cohesion. Some sets of stamps contain irregular shapes and in such cases the usual order of face value (lowest to highest) can be varied, row by row—horizontal designs in one row, verticals on another, or a balanced mixed row, e.g. pairs of horizontal designs flanking vertical ones or vice versa.

Country names or other page headings should be uniform throughout the album, and sufficient space should be left above and below the rows of stamps for sub-headings and captions if it is your intention to write-up the collection. It is generally preferable to complete the written work *before* you mount the stamps (even if you haven't got all of them)—it's tempting fate to write with pen and ink over and across the stamps. And of course if you prefer to use a typewriter then you obviously do your typing first. Measure the length of typed words on a piece of scrap paper so that your captions won't overrun the prescribed length: you can extend the wording to two or three shorter lines. All this preparation is tedious, but ultimately rewarding.

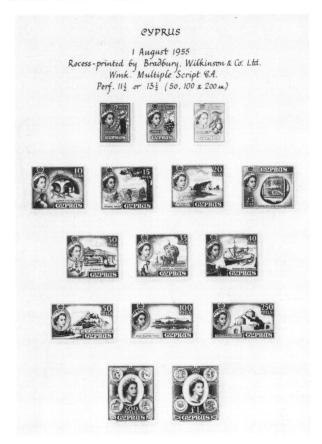

28 A well written up
page of Cyprus stamps

BRANCHING OUT

If, like the apprentice who finally qualifies in his trade, you wish to develop
your stamp collection on more specific lines than simply accumulating
stamps, there are various ways in which you can pursue a serious philatelic
study. The specialist is a mature student of stamps, their design and printing,
their history and postal significance, devoting his attention to one particular
country, or even to one period of a country's issues, its postal history and
postmarks. It follows that a good knowledge of the four principal methods of
printing stamps—recess or line-engraving, typography or 'letterpress',
lithography and photogravure (a form of recess printing)—is one of the
necessary qualifications to becoming a philatelist.

The source of a stamp design is a line-drawing, a watercolour sketch or a
photograph, depending on the printing process contemplated. In recess
printing (the process employed in printing the world's first postage stamps,
the G.B. Penny Black and Twopence Blue of 1840), a line-drawing of the

design subject is engraved, stamp-size, on to a steel or copper die—the 'master die'—which is reproduced on a printing plate or cylinder as many times as required to form a sheet of stamps. The elements of the design comprises recesses and cuts which are inked prior to printing. For typographic printing, the design is engraved in relief (as opposed to recess) and the printing plate is composed of moulds ('stereotypes') reproduced from the original die.

Photogravure printing is another form of the recess process, but instead of being copied by the engraver, the original artwork is photographed and transferred in various stages to be etched on the copper printing cylinder. The stamp image is composed of tiny recesses or 'cells' which vary in depth according to the intensity of colour required on the printed stamps, and which appear as tiny dots. Multicoloured stamps are printed from several cylinders, one for each colour. The photo-lithographic process is the modern version of lithography (or 'offset'), a form of surface printing invented in 1796. The design is photographed on to a zinc plate and outlined in a greasy ink—liberal sprays of water ensure that only the design image is inked, whence a rubber roller or 'blanket' transfers or 'offsets' the stamp designs on to the paper.

29 Fiji stamp showing design error— unmanned boat!

Errors in design and varieties of flaws caused by mishaps in the course of printing are keenly sought by many collectors. The stamp designer may make a simple mistake of identity, motif, caption or time-scale, such as the instances of Columbus using a telescope (not then invented) on a St. Kitts-Nevis stamp, Fiji's unmanned canoe in full sail across a lagoon, and Schubert's music on an East German stamp honouring Schumann. Spelling errors are common and one recalls 'Wakatipu' appearing (incorrectly) as 'Wakitipu' on a New Zealand stamp, and 'Jesselton' shown in error as 'Jessleton' on a North Borneo (Sabah) issue. Errors of colour, colours and parts of a design omitted and 'upside-down' stamps are among the most spectacular printing varieties. Europe's rarest stamp, the Sweden 3-skilling-banco, yellow, is an error of colour—it should have been green and only one is known.

The head of Queen Victoria is known inverted on an Indian 4-annas stamp of 1854, her statue inverted on a Jamaica 1s. stamp of 1920, and the head of Queen Elizabeth II omitted on stamps issued in Great Britain for National Productivity Year in 1962 (3d. and 1s. 3d.). There are also some well-known errors of perforation and watermark. The most common flaws and varieties these days are usually allied to the photogravure printing process—usually blemishes which appear as white patches or spots, extraneous marks or misplaced colours on the stamps. Varieties which occur on the same stamp on every sheet are regarded as 'constant', which gives them a certain status. Most of the worthwhile Elizabethan ones are listed and illustrated in the *Elizabethan Specialised Stamp Catalogue*.

30 A Travelling Post Office postmark

Postal history is concerned with the origins and development of the postal services from earliest times. It involves the study of postal rates, routes and postmarks of a specific area which is of especial interest to the collector. The postmark, as a record of transport routes and dates, is the key to most aspects of postal history, and some collectors make a study of the different postmark types and their uses, supported by covers and other mail items. British stamps 'used abroad' have a special attraction. Railway enthusiasts look for 'Travelling Post Office' and station cancellations, while those who prefer ships seek mail-boat and 'paquebot' postmarks.

STAMP COLLECTOR'S GLOSSARY

Adhesive	A gummed stamp
Albino	A design impression without colour
Aniline	A fugitive ink or dye
Bisect	Part of a stamp which has been cut in two for separate use
Blind perforation	A perforation which has not been punched out
Block	A group of four or more unseparated stamps
Bogus	A spurious, pretended stamp
Booklet	A small, official book of stamps

Cover of Guernsey
stamp booklet

Booklet pane   A leaf of stamps from a booklet

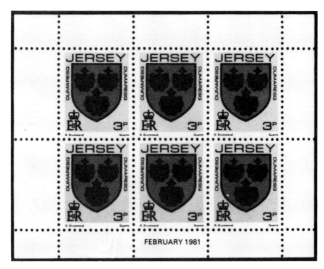

Booklet pane of
Jersey stamps

Cachet	A commemorative inscription
Cancellation	Any authorised defacing mark on a stamp

Centre	The position of a stamp design within its perforations e.g. 'well-centred' or 'off-centre'
Chalky paper	Stamp paper coated with a chalky solution for security purposes. Attempted removal of the postmark damages the surface of the stamp
Charity stamp	One bearing a premium or surcharge for charitable purposes
Classic	A country's early stamp issues up to about 1875; a choice stamp
Coil stamp	One from a roll of stamps used in vending machines
Coil join	A tab uniting two sections of a roll of stamps
Comb perforation	One or several rows of stamps in a sheet perforated top and sides in one stroke
Commemorative	A stamp issued to mark a special anniversary or event
Controls	Letters/numerals appearing in the sheet margins of British stamps (discontinued in 1947)
Cover	A postally used envelope, letter-sheet or wrapper
Cylinder number	Letters/numerals in sheet margins identifying printing cylinders. Normally collected in 'Cylinder block' of six or eight stamps.

33 Cylinder block of Machin 4p stamps

Definitive	A normal stamp for regular use, i.e. not a commemorative
Die	An engraved plate for impressing design etc. on soft metal
Doctor blade	A steel blade which removes surplus ink from the printing cylinder in the press
Embossing	A form of printing in relief, employing male and female dies
Entire	A *complete* letter-sheet or wrapper
Error	A mistake in stamp design, printing or production

Essay	A trial stamp design, differing in some detail from the issued stamps
Face value	The denomination of a stamp, expressed on its face
Fake	A genuine stamp doctored in some way to deceive collectors
First Day Cover	A cover bearing stamps postmarked on their day of issue

34 First Day Cover of modern Netherlands stamps

Flaw	A fortuitous blemish on a stamp; a printing fault
Forgery	A fraudulent copy of a genuine postage stamp, overprint or postmark.
Frank	Endorsement of 'free' postage. Stamped letters are also said to be 'franked'
Graphite lines	Black vertical lines printed on the back of G.B. definitives, 1957–1959, for use with automatic letter-sorting equipment. Also see 'Phosphor' stamps
Gum	Mucilage on the back of adhesive stamps. Not 'glue'
Gutter	The narrow space between stamps in the sheet permitting perforation
Gutter margin	The blank margins dividing a sheet of stamps into panes
Handstamp	A postmark or overprint applied by hand
Imperforate	Stamps printed and issued without perforations
Imprint	The name of the printer or issuing authority inscribed on the stamps or in the sheet margins

Imprinted stamps   Stamps other than adhesives printed direct on post
stationery

35 Printer's imprint in
sheet margin and at
foot of stamp
(designer's name also
shown)

36 Imprinted stamp on
a P.O. postcard

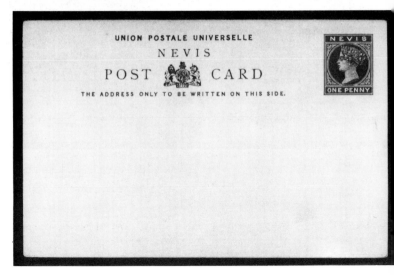

'Invert'	The central design ('vignette') or portion of a stamp printed upside-down in relation to the frame, or vice versa
Line perforation	Perforation of a sheet of stamps by a single line or row of holes—the simplest form of perforation
'Local'	A stamp with geographical limits of postal use and validity. These are not normally listed in the Stanley Gibbons Catalogues
'Machin'	The name given to G.B. definitives, first issued

1967, bearing the Queen's head designed by Arnold Machin

Margin The unprinted edging surrounding or dividing a sheet of stamps. See also 'Gutter margin'

Miniature sheet A small sheet of one or several stamps, usually with decorative margins, issued as a souvenir for collectors

37 Miniature sheet from Sweden

SVENSK FILMHISTORIA 1

PRIS: 10 KRONOR

Mint A stamp in its original pristine state, with full gum (if so issued), when it is said to have its 'original gum' ('O.G.'). 'Unmounted' mint is an unnecessary qualification. Also see 'Unused'

Obsolete A stamp which has ceased to be available for postal use, though maybe still valid for postage

Overprint A printed addition to a stamp. Also see 'Surcharge'

Pair Two unseparated stamps, joined as originally issued

Pane A formation or group of stamps within the sheet. Also see 'Booklet pane'

Perforations Holes punched between stamps in sheets to ease separation

Phosphor stamps Stamps overprinted or coated with phosphorescent materials which 'fluoresce' in electronic letter-facing machines

Plate number Letters/numerals in sheet margins identifying printing plates

Postmark Any mark cancelling the stamp and recording an item's passage through the mails

38 Strip of three
showing plate
number (1) and
printer's imprint

Proof	A trial impression taken from an original die o printing plate
Provisional	A stamp, usually overprinted or surcharged, issued fo temporary use
Remainders	Stamps remaining in official stocks after becoming obsolete
Reprints	Stamps printed anew after being withdrawn. The printing of additional supplies of current stamps is bes described as 'new printings'
Roulette	Stamps separated by a series of cuts instead o perforations
Self-adhesive	Gummed stamps (with protective cover) which do no require moistening
Se-tenant	Stamps of different design or face value etc. joinee together

39 Definitive stamps in
se-tenant arrangement
from Stanley Gibbons
stamp booklet of 1982
(*Reduced*)

40 A *se-tenant* pair—British 1975 Architectural Heritage stamps

Specimen	Sample stamp usually with 'specimen' overprinted or perforated on it
Strip	Three or more stamps joined in a row
Surcharge	An overprint which specifically changes a stamp's face value
Tête-bêche	A stamp inverted in relation to the adjoining stamp in a pair
Unused	An uncancelled stamp, not necessarily 'mint'
Used	A stamp which has been postally used and appropriately postmarked
Used abroad	Stamps of one country used and postmarked in another

41 Surcharged stamp from New Zealand—amending face value from 10c to 14c

42 Variety-misplaced brown colour on 1960 Europa stamp

Variety	A stamp differing in some detail from the normal issue
Vignette	The central portion of a stamp design, printed separately within the frame; strictly one which shades off at its edges
Watermark	A distinctive device or emblem in stamps, formed by 'thinning' of the paper during production. A watermark is normally viewed through the *front* of the stamp
'Wilding'	The name given to British definitive stamps, issued between 1952 and about 1967, bearing the Queen's head from a portrait by Dorothy Wilding

43 British 'Wilding' stamp—2d brown first issued in 1953

USEFUL ADDRESSES

British Philatelic Federation, 314 Vauxhall Bridge Rd,
LONDON SW1V 1AA   Tel. 01-828 4416

British Post Office Philatelic Bureau, 20 Brandon St,
EDINBURGH EH3 9TT   Tel. 031-556 8661

Philatelic Sales Counters are provided at the London Chief Post Office (King Edward St, London EC1) and the Trafalgar Square Branch Office (William IV St, London WC2) and at the main post offices in the following towns: Ayr Ballymena, Belfast, Birmingham, Blackpool, Bournemouth, Brighton Bristol, Cambridge, Canterbury, Cardiff, Chester, Colchester, Coventry Croydon, Edinburgh, Exeter, Glasgow, Gloucester, Guildford, Harrogate Hereford, Hull, Inverness, Leeds, Leicester, Liverpool, Manchester Middlesbrough, Milton Keynes, Newcastle-upon-Tyne, Newport (Gwent) Newry, Northampton, Norwich, Nottingham, Oldham, Oxford, Ports mouth, Plymouth, Romford, Sheffield, Shrewsbury, Southampton Southend-on-Sea, Stoke-on-Trent, Swansea, Swindon, Truro, Windsor Worcester and York.

The addresses can be found in local telephone directories. Other counters may be opened later.

Stanley Gibbons Ltd, 399 Strand,
LONDON WC2R 0LX   Tel. 01-836 8444

Shop Hours: Monday–Friday 9.30 am–5.30 pm.
Saturday 10.00 am–12.30 pm.

The *Gibbons Gallery* hold regular displays of fine or unusual stamps and postal history. Details of the exhibitions are given in *Gibbons Stamp Monthly* The Gallery is open Monday to Saturday, closing 30 minutes before the shop admission is free.

National Philatelic Society, 27 King St,
LONDON WC2E 8JD   Tel. 01-240 7349

National Postal Museum, King Edward St,
LONDON EC1A 1LP   Tel. 01-432 3851

Opening hours: 10.00 am.–4.30 pm. Monday–Thursday, 10.00 am.–4.00 pm Friday, admission is free.

(Post Office) Stamp Bug Club (*for young collectors*), Freepost,
P.O. Box 109, Baker St., HIGH WYCOMBE, Bucks. HP11 2TD